Counting with Sebastian Pig and Friends On the Farm

By Jill Anderson

Illustrated by Amy Huntington

Series Math Consultant:
Cassi Heppelmann
Elementary School Teacher
Farmington School District
Minnesota

Series Literacy Consultant:
Allan A. De Fina, Ph.D.
Dean, College of Education / Professor of Literacy Education
New Jersey City University
Past President of the New Jersey Reading Association

Enslow Elementary
an imprint of

Enslow Publishers, Inc.
40 Industrial Road
Box 398
Berkeley Heights, NJ 07922
USA

http://www.enslow.com

To Parents and Teachers:

As you read Sebastian's story with a child,

   *Rely on the pictures to see the math visually represented.

   *Use Sebastian's notebook, which summarizes the math at hand.

   *Practice math facts with your child using the charts at the end of this book.

Enslow Elementary, an imprint of Enslow Publishers, Inc.

Enslow Elementary® is a registered trademark of Enslow Publishers, Inc.

Copyright © 2009 by Enslow Publishers, Inc.

Library of Congress Cataloging-in-Publication Data
Anderson, Jill, 1968-
   Counting with Sebastian pig and friends : on the farm / written by Jill Anderson ; illustrated by Amy Huntington.
      p. cm. — (Math fun with Sebastian pig and friends!)
   Includes index.
   Summary: "Review counting by ones, twos, fives, and tens on a farm with Sebastian Pig"—Provided by publisher.
   ISBN-13: 978-0-7660-3359-7
   ISBN-10: 0-7660-3359-7
   1. Counting—Juvenile literature. I. Title.
   QA113.A56537 2009
   513.2'11—dc22
                    2008028469

Editorial Direction: Red Line Editorial, Inc.

Printed in the United States of America

10 9 8 7 6 5 4 3 2 1

Table of Contents

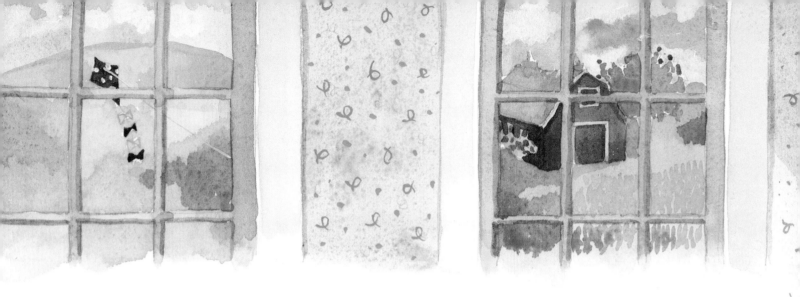

There's trouble at Farmer Frank's farm. Sebastian needs
to find the bad guy—fast! He will count all the animals
on the farm. He will find the one who does not belong.

Let's help Sebastian! Count by ones, twos, fives, and tens.
Look in Sebastian's notebook for help. Look at the pictures, too.

Trouble on the Farm

Help! Someone has painted spots on Farmer Frank's barn!

"I know how to find him!" Sebastian Pig says. The farm has 100 animals. He will count them all. He will find the one who should not be there.

One, Two . . . Too Slow!

"One, two, three, four." Sebastian counts the cats in the tree.

"Oh no," he says. "Counting a few cats is easy. But counting to 100 will take forever!

"I know! Counting by twos will be faster."

Two by Two

"WATCH OUT!" someone calls out. Sebastian steps out of the way. Dogs run by.

Sebastian counts again, this time by twos. First he counts four cats. Then he adds the dogs.

Count by twos!

1 2 **2**

3 4 **4**

5 6 **6**

7 8 **8**

Whooosh! The ducks play in the water.

Sebastian adds them to his count. Now he is getting somewhere!

More animal pairs

1 2		2
3 4		4
5 6		6
7 8		8
9 10		10
11 12		12

14

Up to 20

1 2		**2**
3 4		**4**
5 6		**6**
7 8		**8**
9 10		**10**
11 12		**12**
13 14		**14**
15 16		**16**
17 18		**18**
19 20		**20**

The chickens zip by. "Just try and count us," they say.

Sebastian counts them by twos.

Wait a minute. Is he only up to 20? He needs to find a faster way. What if he counts by fives?

Count by fives!

1	2	3	4	5	5
6	7	8	9	10	10
11	12	13	14	15	15
16	17	18	19	20	20
21	22	23	24	25	25
26	27	28	29	30	30

Faster by Fives

Next Sebastian sees the geese. They are busy painting. He counts them by fives. Where is he now? He is at 30!

The cows get haircuts. Sebastian is happy he does not need one. But he wants to go fast.

Sebastian counts by fives. Then he runs out the door.

More rows of five

1	2	3	4	5	5
6	7	8	9	10	10
11	12	13	14	15	15
16	17	18	19	20	20
21	22	23	24	25	25
26	27	28	29	30	30
31	32	33	34	35	35
36	37	38	39	40	40

MOO CUTS!

MOOVIE STARS

MOO Fashion MAGAZINE

Halfway to 100

Zooooom! Rabbits race along the road!

Sebastian counts them as fast as he can. But he is still only at 50. How can he count faster?

"I know!" he says. "Next time I'll count by tens!"

Terrific by Ten

Sebastian hears singing. No way! The Goo Goo Pigs are singing tonight!

Sebastian goes to watch the Goo Goo Pigs. Counting them by tens is so much fun. Sebastian stays to hear a song.

Count by tens!

Sebastian sees the horses next. They are playing chess.
They do not look up at Sebastian as he counts them.

More rows of ten

1	2	3	4	5	6	7	8	9	10	**10**
11	12	13	14	15	16	17	18	19	20	**20**
21	22	23	24	25	26	27	28	29	30	**30**
31	32	33	34	35	36	37	38	39	40	**40**
41	42	43	44	45	46	47	48	49	50	**50**
51	52	53	54	55	56	57	58	59	60	**60**
61	62	63	64	65	66	67	68	69	70	**70**
71	72	73	74	75	76	77	78	79	80	**80**

One Too Many!

At the last stop, Sebastian sees sheep. They are in rows of ten. Sebastian starts to count. Wait! Sebastian starts counting again. "80, 90, 100 . . . and AHA! 101!" There is an extra animal in the last row. It is not a sheep. It is a calf!

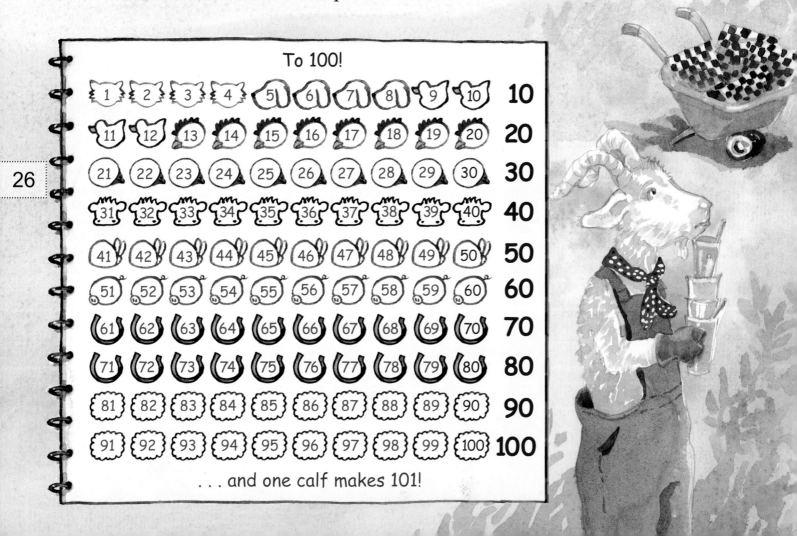

To 100!

1	2	3	4	5	6	7	8	9	10	**10**
11	12	13	14	15	16	17	18	19	20	**20**
21	22	23	24	25	26	27	28	29	30	**30**
31	32	33	34	35	36	37	38	39	40	**40**
41	42	43	44	45	46	47	48	49	50	**50**
51	52	53	54	55	56	57	58	59	60	**60**
61	62	63	64	65	66	67	68	69	70	**70**
71	72	73	74	75	76	77	78	79	80	**80**
81	82	83	84	85	86	87	88	89	90	**90**
91	92	93	94	95	96	97	98	99	100	**100**

. . . and one calf makes 101!

"Here is the bad guy, Farmer Frank," Sebastian says.

Farmer Frank smiles. "I can always count on you, Sebastian Pig!"

Now You Know

You helped Sebastian find the bad guy! Now practice counting to 100 on your own.

Use all the numbers to count by ones up to 100. Use just the **red** numbers to count by twos.

1	2	3	4	5	6	7	8	9	10
11	12	13	14	15	16	17	18	19	20
21	22	23	24	25	26	27	28	29	30
31	32	33	34	35	36	37	38	39	40
41	42	43	44	45	46	47	48	49	50
51	52	53	54	55	56	57	58	59	60
61	62	63	64	65	66	67	68	69	70
71	72	73	74	75	76	77	78	79	80
81	82	83	84	85	86	87	88	89	90
91	92	93	94	95	96	97	98	99	100

Use the green numbers to count by fives up to 100. Did you notice how all the green numbers end in a 5 or a 0?

1	2	3	4	5	6	7	8	9	10
11	12	13	14	15	16	17	18	19	20
21	22	23	24	25	26	27	28	29	30
31	32	33	34	35	36	37	38	39	40
41	42	43	44	45	46	47	48	49	50
51	52	53	54	55	56	57	58	59	60
61	62	63	64	65	66	67	68	69	70
71	72	73	74	75	76	77	78	79	80
81	82	83	84	85	86	87	88	89	90
91	92	93	94	95	96	97	98	99	100

Counting to 100 by tens goes really fast. Try it using the blue numbers. What is special about all these numbers?

1	2	3	4	5	6	7	8	9	10
11	12	13	14	15	16	17	18	19	20
21	22	23	24	25	26	27	28	29	30
31	32	33	34	35	36	37	38	39	40
41	42	43	44	45	46	47	48	49	50
51	52	53	54	55	56	57	58	59	60
61	62	63	64	65	66	67	68	69	70
71	72	73	74	75	76	77	78	79	80
81	82	83	84	85	86	87	88	89	90
91	92	93	94	95	96	97	98	99	100

Learn More

Books

Curious George Learns to Count from 1 to 100. Boston: Houghton Mifflin, 2005.

Murphy, Patricia J. *Counting Puppies and Kittens*. Berkeley Heights, NJ: Enslow Publishers, 2008.

Murphy, Stuart J. *Leaping Lizards*. New York: HarperCollins, 2005.

Web Sites

FunBrain
http://www.funbrain.com/numbers.html

Cool Math
http://www.coolmath4kids.com

Index